GOD'S PURPOSE IN CREATION:

A Study in Genesis 1

INSTITUTE FOR
FAITH, WORK
& ECONOMICS

First Edition, 2015

ISBN 978-0-9964257-2-8

Published by the

Institute for Faith, Work & Economics

8400 Westpark Drive

Suite 100

McLean, Virginia 22102

www.tifwe.org

Printed in the United States of America

ABOUT THE INSTITUTE
FOR FAITH, WORK & ECONOMICS

The Institute for Faith, Work & Economics™ (IFWE) is a non-profit, 501(c)(3) Christian research organization committed to promoting biblical and economic principles that help individuals find fulfillment in their work and contribute to a free and flourishing society.

IFWE's research starts with the belief that the Bible, as the inerrant Word of God, provides the authoritative and intellectual foundation for a proper understanding of work and economic truths that, when properly followed, can help individuals, companies, communities, and nations flourish.

IFWE's research is based on three core principles:

- Each person is created in God's image and, like him, has a desire to be creative and to find **fulfillment** using their God-given talents through work.
- All work, whether paid or volunteer, matters to God, and we as Christians are called to pursue excellence throughout the week – not just on Sundays – stewarding all that we've been given for God's glory and for the **flourishing** of society.
- Therefore, we as citizens must promote an economic environment that not only provides us the **freedom** to pursue our callings and flourish in our work but also reflects the inherent dignity of every human being.

Our desire is to help Christians view their work within the bigger picture of what God is doing in the world. Not only do we help Christians find personal fulfillment, but we also help them understand how to better alleviate poverty, address greed, and view possessions properly. With a biblical view of work and economics, we can partner together to be meaningful participants in God's plan to restore the world the way he intended it to be.

We invite you to learn more though our other resources:

- Our blog *Creativity, Purpose, Freedom* provides brief but powerful insights
- Our book *How Then Should We Work* is a perfect starting point for understanding the biblical meaning of work
- Our white papers offer concise explanations of our most significant research and findings
- Request a speaker to share these ideas at your next event
- Sign up for our newsletter and receive updates on our latest events and publications

The Mission of God's People

Genesis 1:1

Far too often Christians think, as Dr. Richard Pratt says, "Jesus came to forgive our sin, make our souls sparkle, to sprinkle us with peace and joy so we can sprout wings when we die, grab a harp and join the eternal choir."[i]

Nothing could be further from the truth.

God has called each of us from death to life, from darkness into his glorious light for a reason.[ii] Part of that reason is what he wants us to accomplish in the here and now. To know what it is God wants us to do with our lives with the time we have, we must go back to where God's grand story starts – Genesis 1.

Google Genesis 1 and you will get over 200,000,000 hits, most of them dealing with questions like:

- Did God create the world in six ordinary days?
- How should people understand the theory of evolution in light of Genesis 1?
- Were the "days" of Genesis 1 great ages or epochs?
- Are the opening chapters of Genesis to be taken literally?

When Moses wrote the opening chapters of Genesis, he probably was not concerned about these things. Instead he was trying to prepare God's people of his day for the mission they were created to fulfill, a mission we as Christians in the 21st century are still called to accomplish.

Regarding this mission, Christopher J. H. Wright, in his book *The Mission of God's People*, writes,

When God created the earth, he created human beings in his own image with the express mission of ruling over creation by caring for it – a task modeled on the kingship of God himself. The human mission has never been rescinded, and Christians have not been given some exemption on the grounds that we have other or better things to do.[iii]

The author of Genesis is telling his first audience – and us as well – that man's original calling is found in the creation narrative. The gospel call is a redemptive return to a lost and forfeited calling: to being God's image bearers in the world,[iv] a calling that has never had anything less than the entirety of God's original, good creation in view.

Wright puts the issue as clearly and bluntly as possible:

> Creation is not just the disposable backdrop to the lives of human creatures who were really intended to live somewhere else, and some day will do so. We are not redeemed out of creation, but as part of the redeemed creation itself – a creation that will again be fully and eternally for God's glory, for our joy and benefit, forever.[v]

In opening verses of Genesis we see God at work creating the heavens and the earth *ex nihilo*, out of nothing, and that all he had made was good.[vi] It is clear from this creation story that God delights in the work of his hands.

J.R.R. Tolkien called man, made in the image of God, a "sub-creator" and saw this process of sub-creation as a form of worship, a way for creatures to express the divine image in them by creating something out of something. Through our work we are called to be creative and productive, imitating our Creator. We should enjoy not only the work of God's hands, but also that of our own.

Work in different forms is mentioned over 800 times in the Bible, more than all the terms used for worship, music, praise, and singing combined. As we will see throughout this study, work is what we were created to do. It is the work we have been called to do even in our daily vocations that sustains the mission for which we were intended.

"The problem with Western Christians is not that they aren't where they should be, but that they aren't what they should be where they are," writes Os Guinness in his classic book, *The Call*.[vii] We should be on a mission, and that mission is to be who God intended us to be as we live and work in his world for his glory.[viii] ■

REFERENCES

i   Richard L. Pratt, Jr, *Designed for Dignity: What God Has Made It Possible for You to Be* (Phillipsburg: P&R Publishing, 1993).

ii I Pet. 2:9 (NIV).

iii Christopher J.H. Wright, *The Mission of God's People: A Biblical Theology of the Church's Mission* (Grand Rapids: Zondervan, 2010).

iv Ps. 8 (NIV).

v   Wright, *The Mission of God's People*.

vi Gen. 1:4, 1:10, 1:12, 1:18, 1:21, 1:25 (NIV).

vii Os Guinness, *The Call: Finding and Fulfilling the Central Purpose of Your Life* (Nashville: Thomas Nelson, 2003) 166-167.

viii I Cor. 10:31; Col. 3:17, 3:23 (NIV).

Reflection Questions:

1. When you think of the first chapter of the Bible, what comes to mind? How does today's devotional material affect your view of Genesis chapter one?

_____

_____

_____

_____

_____

_____

_____

2. Consider the statement, "Work in different forms is mentioned over 800 times in the Bible, more than all the terms used for worship, music, praise, and singing combined." What is the significance of this fact, and what does it say about our work?

_____

_____

_____

_____

_____

_____

_____

Discussion Questions:

1. What is the mission of God's people?

_____

_____

_____

_____

_____

_____

2. Why is it important to focus on the creation narrative within Genesis 1?

_____

_____

_____

_____

_____

_____

Genesis 1 – The First Chapter of a Larger Story

Genesis 1:3-5

T he first chapter of Genesis is more than the introduction to the first book of the Bible. It is the opening chapter in the grand story of God's redemptive plan[i] for his creation.

This comprehensive story has four parts:
- Creation (the way things were).[ii]
- Fall (the way things are).[iii]
- Redemption (the way things could be).[iv]
- Restoration (the way things will be).[v]

These four parts together are called the four-chapter gospel.

Many Christians today have lost this larger story told by the Bible. Despite the greatness of the biblical narrative, many theologians believe that over the past 150 years the church in the western world has looked at the Bible from a different, more limited perspective. We have truncated the four-chapter gospel down to two chapters, Fall and Redemption. While sin and salvation are undeniable realities, they are not the complete gospel. This abridged version of the gospel leaves out God's original good creation and his future restoration of it.

It is an incomplete story with a number of problems. The two-chapter gospel:
- Does not tell us why we were created.
- Does not tell us about our true destiny.
- Tends to over emphasize the individualistic aspects of salvation. Salvation becomes all about us.
- Tends to lead to an escapist view of redemption.
- Becomes just a gospel of sin management.

This two-chapter gospel often leads Christians today to see their salvation only as a bus ticket to heaven. They believe that what they do while they wait for the bus doesn't really matter. This simply isn't true.

Rather than being mere passengers at a bus stop waiting for the bus, we have a specific mission and identity as God's people. Reading the Bible as one narrative within the framework of the four-chapter gospel enables us to understand that identity as we see our role in God's story. Understanding this comprehensive story's call on our lives enables us to withstand being "conformed to the world."[vi]

From this perspective we clearly see our call to participate in God's redemptive mission. That missional role is not in the future, but in the here and now. By recovering scripture's storyline, we rediscover our true purpose and identity.

The gospel, when understood in its fullness, starts in Genesis 1 with creation. It is not solely about individual happiness and fulfillment. It is not all about "me." Tim Keller says, "It is not just a wonderful plan for 'my life' but a wonderful plan for the world; it is about the coming of God's kingdom to renew all things."[vii] Only with the four-chapter gospel in view can we understand how our story fits into God's story and begin to fulfill his plan for our lives.

Scripture begins with the creation of all things and ends with the renewal of all things. In between it offers an interpretation of the meaning of all history. N.T. Wright says that the divine drama told in Scripture "offers a story which is the story of the whole world. It is public truth."[viii]

The biblical story makes a comprehensive claim on all humanity, calling each one of us to find our place in God's story. ■

REFERENCES

i   Lk 24:25-27 (NIV).

ii   Gen. 1:27-31 (NIV).

iii   Rom. 5:12 (NIV).

iv   Rom. 3:22-26 (NIV).

v   Rev. 22:1-5 (NIV).

vi   Rom. 12:1-2 (NIV).

vii   Timothy Keller, "Our New Global Culture: Ministry in Urban Centers", http://www.copgny.org/files/Movement%20Day/Ministry_In_Urban_Centers.pdf

viii   N.T. Wright, *The New Testament and the People of God: Christian Origins and the Question of God*, Vol. 1 (Minneapolis: Fortress Press, 1992).

Reflection Questions:

1. How does today's material influence your view of the gospel, if at all?

_____

_____

_____

_____

_____

_____

_____

2. Why is it important to view scripture as one cohesive, grand story?

_____

_____

_____

_____

_____

_____

_____

Discussion Questions:

1. What is harmful about viewing the gospel only as Fall and Redemption? What are the benefits to viewing the gospel as Creation, Fall, Redemption, and Restoration?

_____

_____

_____

_____

_____

2. How does the four-chapter gospel inform our role in God's story?

_____

_____

_____

_____

_____

Made in the Image of God

Genesis 1:26-27

N
ear the end of the sixth day of the creation story we read, "Then God said, Let us make mankind in our image, in our likeness."[i] The phrase, "Let us make man in our image" reveals a lot about our own nature and about the nature of God.

Being made in the image of God means we were made to be relational beings.

The orthodox doctrine of the Trinity recognizes that God is one God, co-existing in three distinct persons of the Father, Son, and Holy Spirit. This is clearly taught in the scriptures[ii] and has been recognized by the church since the second and third century. It is also formalized in the early Christian creeds, like the Apostles' Creed and the Nicene Creed. These three persons of the Trinity are forever in perfect relationship with each other. There has always been and always will be absolute love, joy, and peace within the Godhead.

The very essence of God is relational, and that essential quality has been imprinted on us as humans. We were made to be in relationship with the creator and with the rest of his creation.

As professor Darrell Johnson notes in his book *Experiencing the Trinity*,

> At the center of the universe is a relationship. This is the most fundamental truth I know. At the center of the universe is a community. It is out of that relationship that you and I were created and redeemed. And it is for that relationship that you and I were created and redeemed![iii]

Therefore, when we were made in God's image, we were made to be in relationship.

This truth is at the very heart of the gospel. The universe in which we live was created by a good and gracious heavenly father who filled it with good things to enjoy and moral laws by which to structure to our lives.

The chief goal of life is neither to enjoy the good gifts, nor obey the laws, but to know and be known by the Creator.[iv] This loving relationship between God and man is the way things are supposed to be. Our purpose, fulfillment, delight, and very life itself flow from this relationship with him. As the famous passage from St. Augustine's *Confessions* reads, "You have made us for yourself, O Lord, and our heart is restless until it rests in you."[v]

Andy Crouch writes in his book *Culture Making* that God created a world, "designed for the flourishing of exquisitely relational creatures, male and female, who themselves are very good because they bear the image of a relational God."[vi]

While God created us to be in relationship with him, he also created us to be in relationship with one another.[vii] This interconnectedness plays an important part in God's design for his creation and his desire for it to flourish.

While we are all made in God's image, we are also uniquely made. This is not an accident. It is an important part of God's plan for us and his creation.

Our culture stresses the importance of independence, but the Bible teaches *inter*dependence[viii] and emphasizes community. The Apostle Paul makes this very clear in I Corinthians 12 when he reminds the Corinthian church that we are not made to do everything by ourselves. Paul's beautiful illustration of the unity of the human body establishes that while we are each uniquely created with different combinations of gifts and talents, we are to use these personal resources in relationship with others. As we each do what we are best at doing, together we all add much more to the common good than we could alone. This is what God intended from the beginning.

Our relationships and creativity, like all things in creation, were damaged by the Fall. It is through Christ's redemption that we are restored to a right relationship with our heavenly father and each other. That in turn allows Christians to seek the fullness and wholeness of living and being good, creative stewards in community. When we do this, we bring a new level of flourishing to our families and our communities through our work, which reflects the glory of God to a world that is in desperate need of finding something greater.

Adam was created to bear God's image into the world. He was created to perform a task. Image bearing was his reason for being and his very identity. Thus the language of image bearing in scripture bears a dynamic, active, functional trajectory. "God has created us in his image," says biblical scholar Anthony Hoekema, "so that we may carry out a task, fulfill a mission, pursue a calling."[ix] The point of image bearing in scripture is obedience to God's will by serving him and our fellow man. ■

REFERENCES

i Gen. 1:26 (NIV).

ii I Jn 5:7; Matt. 3:16-17, 28:19; Jn. 14:16-17, 14:23 (NIV).

iii Darrell W. Johnson, *Experiencing the Trinity* (British Columbia: Regent College Publishing, 2002).

iv James 4:6-10; Jn. 14:6-9; Hosea 6:6 (NIV).

v Augustine, *Confessions*, trans. Henry Chadwick (Oxford: Oxford Paperbacks, 2009).

vi Andy Crouch, *Culture Making: Recovering Our Creative Calling* (Westmont: Intervarsity Press, 2013).

vii Mt. 22:36-40 (NIV).

viii Rom. 12:4-5 (NIV).

ix Anthony A. Hoekema, *Created in God's Image* (Grand Rapids: Eerdman's, 1986), 73.

Reflection Questions:

1. What connection do you see between being made in God's image and your work?

_____

_____

_____

_____

_____

_____

_____

Discussion Questions:

1. How does community relate to being made in God's image?

_____

_____

_____

_____

_____

_____

Discussion Questions continued:

2. What does the importance of community mean for the mission of God's people?

NOTES:

Man's First Calling –
The Culture Mandate
Genesis 1:28-30, Genesis 9:1

"God has created us in his image so that we may carry out a task, fulfill a mission, pursue a calling," writes Anthony A. Hoekema, in his book *Created in God's Image*.[i] In the opening chapter of Genesis, we hear God describe the purpose for which he created man:

> Then God said, "Let us make mankind in our image, in our likeness, so that they may rule over the fish in the sea and the birds in the sky, over the livestock and all the wild animals, and over all the creatures that move along the ground."[ii]

In the next verse he relates this mission statement to Adam and Eve:

> God blessed them and said to them, be fruitful and increase in number; fill the earth and subdue it. Rule over the fish in the sea and the birds in the sky and over every living creature that moves on the ground.[iii]

This passage, often called the *cultural mandate*, calls all Christians to partner with God in his work. The cultural mandate calls us to fill the earth with God's images and subdue it.

Writing about this passage in her book *Total Truth*, Nancy Pearcey explains:

> The first phrase "be fruitful and multiply," means to develop the social world: build families, churches, schools, cities, governments, laws. The second phrase, "subdue the earth," means to harness the natural world: plant crops, build bridges, design computers, and compose music. This passage is sometimes called the Cultural Mandate because it tells us that our original purpose was to create cultures, build civilizations–nothing less.[iv]

The significance of all of our work, in our jobs, our homes, our communities, and our churches, is directly related to its connection with God's work. Pearcey writes:

> The lesson of the Cultural Mandate is that our sense of fulfillment depends on engaging in creative, constructive work. The ideal human existence is not eternal leisure or an endless vacation – or even a monastic retreat into prayer and meditation – but creative effort expended for the glory of God and the benefit of others.[v]

The Garden of Eden was perfect but not finished. Adam and Eve would not have stayed there forever, even if they had never fallen into sin. Following the commands of the cultural mandate, they would have moved out into the world, filling it with God's images and subduing it. The Hebrew word translated "subdue" in verse 28 (Hebrew *kabash*) literally means to make the earth useful for human beings' benefit and enjoyment.[vi]

The idea behind cultural mandate is that God entrusts us with something and expects us to do something worthwhile with it, something he finds valuable. This mandate implies an expectation of human achievement.

Richard Pratt's claim that "God ordained humanity to be the primary instrument by which his kingship will be realized on earth"[vii] leads him to a down-to-earth description of how the cultural mandate works:

> The Great King has summoned each of us into his throne room. Take this portion of my kingdom, he says, I am making you my steward over your office, your workbench, your kitchen stove. Put your heart into mastering this part of my world. Get it in order; unearth its treasures; do all you can with it. Then everyone will see what a glorious King I am. That's why we get up every morning and go to work. We don't labor simply to survive, insects do that. Our work is an honor, a privileged commission from our great King. God has given each of us a portion of his kingdom to explore and to develop to its fullness.[viii]

It is the gospel of Christ that brings us back to this first calling. As biblical scholar Michael Williams writes:

> The first calling of the biblical story is a calling to the world, a calling that comes for the sake of God's purpose to bless all things that he has made. And this calling informs and shapes the people of God throughout the entirety of the biblical story. Should we miss our first calling, a calling that informs the nature and purpose of our very existence, we will in fact impoverish the biblical portrayal of calling.[ix]

This calling is what we were made to do. It is where we will find purpose and fulfillment. ■

REFERENCES

i Hoekema, *Created in God's Image*, 73.

ii Gen. 1:26 (NIV).

iii Gen. 1:28 (NIV).

iv Nancy Pearcey, *Total Truth: Liberating Christianity from Its Cultural Captivity* (Wheaton: Crossway, 2008), 47.

v Pearcey, *Total Truth*, 49.

vi Wayne Grudem and Barry Asmus, *The Poverty of Nations: A Sustainable Solution* (Wheaton: Crossway, 2013).

vii Pratt, *Designed for Dignity*, 7.

viii Pratt, *Designed for Dignity*, 32-33.

ix Michael D. Williams, "First Calling: The Imago Dei and the Order of Creation", Covenant Seminary, https://www.covenantseminary.edu/the-thistle/first-calling/

Reflection Questions:

1. In Genesis 1:28-30 God gave Adam work to do before the Fall. How does this affect the way we view work?

_____

_____

_____

_____

_____

_____

_____

2. How can the cultural mandate bring you a sense of purpose and fulfillment?

_____

_____

_____

_____

_____

_____

Discussion Questions:

1. How does the cultural mandate affect how we view our work in family life, in church, in community, and in our vocations?

_____

_____

_____

_____

_____

_____

_____

2. What does it mean to say the Garden of Eden was not complete in Genesis 1? What does this mean for our understanding of work?

_____

_____

_____

_____

_____

_____

Man's Job Decription – The Culture Mandate, Part Two
Genesis 1:28-30, Jeremiah 29:4-7

On the sixth day of creation, God comes to Adam and Eve and gives them their job description, "God blessed them and said to them, 'Be fruitful and increase in number; fill the earth and subdue it.'"[i]

Nancy Pearcey writes in her book, *Total Truth*:

> The lesson of the Cultural Mandate is that our sense of fulfillment depends on engaging in creative, constructive work. The ideal human existence is not eternal leisure or an endless vacation—or even a monastic retreat into prayer and meditation—but creative effort expended for the glory of God and the benefit of others. Our calling is not just to "go to heaven" but also to cultivate the earth, not just to "save souls" but also to serve God through our work. For God himself is engaged not only in the work of salvation but also in the work of preserving and developing His creation. When we obey the Cultural Mandate, we participate in the work of God himself. Our role is a call for man to work with and for God The cultural mandate was meant not only for Adam and Eve, but for us as well. It still stands as God's directive for our stewardship of his creation.[ii]

Tragically, because of sin introduced during the Fall, men and women have abused their stewardship of God's creation, lost their sense of the cultural mandate, and struggle to find purpose and fulfillment. But Christians, because of Christ's redemptive work in their lives, now stand in the same place as Adam and Eve before the Fall. They not only know what God wants them to do, but they are also equipped by the Holy Spirit to fulfill this calling.

They can now approach their work in their families, their church, their communities, and their vocations with a clear understanding of God's mandate. They are now called and empowered to begin again to exercise proper stewardship over God's creation.

The prophet Jeremiah understood this, and when writing to the Israelites, who were in exiled in Babylon, reminded them of the cultural mandate:

> Marry and have sons and daughters; find wives for your sons and give your daughters in marriage, so that they too may have sons and daughters. Increase in number there; do not decrease. Also, seek the peace and prosperity of the city to which I have carried you into exile. Pray to the Lord for it, because if it prospers, you too will prosper.[iii]

Jeremiah is telling them to remember that although they are in a strange land living under adverse circumstances, they are still to continue to fill the earth with God's images and subdue it.

Interestingly, Jeremiah describes subduing the earth as a type of biblical flourishing which is both missional and outward focused, motivated on spreading God's glory throughout the earth.

This mandate is still in force today. As the vice-regents of God, we are to bring God's truth and God's will to bear on every sphere of our world and our society. We are to exercise godly dominion and influence over our neighborhoods, our schools, our government, our literature and arts, our sports arenas, our entertainment media, our news media, our scientific endeavors, and every other aspect and institution of human society.

"God commanded Adam and Eve to be fruitful, to multiply, to fill the earth, and to subdue it for God's glory. Jesus, the second Adam, has taken up that task. Just as the first Adam had a bride to serve as his helper, so the second Adam has chosen a bride to serve as his helper," writes John Fesko.[iv]

The bride of Jesus is the church[v]. Together with his bride, Jesus is fulfilling the original mandate by filling the earth with regenerated images of God, who in turn submit to God's rule and subdue the earth for his glory.

The cultural mandate was meant to govern everything Adam and Eve would do after it was given, and it governs everything we do as Christians today. As the social critic Herbert Schlossberg says in his book, *Idols for Destruction*, "The 'salt' of people changed by the gospel must change the world."[vi]

The gospel calls all Christians to be faithful to God's mission as expressed in the cultural mandate. Richard Pratt sums it up this way in his book *Designed for Dignity*, "By filling and ruling over the world, we fulfill our true purpose in life. We reach the heights of dignity because we represent and extend the authority of the King of the universe."[vii] ■

REFERENCES

i   Gen. 1:28 (NIV).

ii   Pearcy, *Total Truth*.

iii Jer. 29:6-7 (NIV).

iv   J.V. Fesko, *Last Things First: Unlocking Genesis with the Christ of Eschatology* (San Clemente: Mentor, 2007).

v   Eph. 5:29-32 (NIV).

vi   Herbert Schlossberg, *Idols for Destruction: The Conflict of Christian Faith and American Culture* (Wheaton: Crossway, 1993) 324.

vii Pratt, *Designed for Dignity*, 27.

Reflection Question:

1. Do you struggle to find purpose and fulfillment in your work?

_____

_____

_____

_____

_____

_____

_____

Discussion Questions:

1. What does the cultural mandate mean for the church?

_____

_____

_____

_____

_____

_____

Discussion Questions continued:

2. How can we be inspired by the cultural mandate?

_____

_____

_____

_____

_____

_____

NOTES:

_____

_____

_____

_____

_____

_____

_____

_____

_____

God's Purpose in Creation
Genesis 1:31, Revelation 4:11

As we look at the first five days of creation in the first chapter of Genesis, we read four times, "And God saw that it was good."[i] Yet, at the end of the sixth day we read, "God saw all that he had made, and it was *very* good.[ii]

Why is there this difference on the sixth day?

At the end of his work of creation, at the end of the sixth day, God was delighted with all of his work. It gave him great pleasure when he surveyed all he had made. Everything worked together exactly as he planned, from the smallest subatomic particles to the largest galaxies spinning in space. There was a "very good," complex interdependency running throughout the whole of creation.

John Schneider writes in his book, *The Good of Affluence,*

> This creation that God majestically called forth into being is good. It is good in its individual parts, and it is good as a whole, as an integrated system. In fact, in this integrative cosmic sense, the text informs us that God declared it to be very good.[iii]

We read in the book of Revelation that the purpose of the creation is to glorify the creator:

> You are worthy, O Lord, to receive glory and honor and power: for you have created all things, and for your pleasure they are and were created.[iv]

God is most glorified when his creation works like it was designed to work. This idea is epitomized by the Old Testament idea of *shalom.* Cornelius Plantinga in his book, *Not the Way It's Supposed to Be,* defines shalom as:

> The webbing together of God, humans, and all creation in justice, fulfillment, and delight…Shalom means universal flourishing, wholeness and delight – a rich state of affairs in which natural needs are satisfied and natural gifts fruitfully employed, Shalom, in other words, is the way things ought to be…the full flourishing of human life in all aspects, as God intended it to be.[v]

Just as a great painting reflects the glory of the master artist, creation reflects the glory of God. This is another reason why God describes his creation as "very good."

The gospel of Christ empowers us as Christians to be faithful to God's original calling as expressed in the cultural mandate. We reweave *shalom* within our spheres of influence by exercising stewardship, by subduing the earth and making it useful for the benefit and enjoyment of human beings. In other words, we bring about flourishing by obeying the cultural mandate. We move the world back to the way it should be when we carry out this mandate through our work.

Jesus Christ is our model for reweaving *shalom* on this earth through stewardship. His life is the ultimate example of giving people a glimpse of how things could be – of what creation might be when it is restored in the new heavens and new earth.

Scripture tells us that during his ministry on earth, Jesus healed the blind man. He fed the five thousand and performed many other miracles. Did Jesus heal everyone that was sick in Israel? Did he feed everyone that was hungry? No, he did not. Could he have? Of course.

As the Son of God, he could have done anything he wanted to do. Why didn't he? Some theologians suggest that he was demonstrating his power and authority in these signs and wonders. This is correct, but there is another reason.

Jesus's time on earth, like ours, takes place within the third chapter of the grand story of the Bible, the four-chapter gospel. This third chapter, Redemption, explains "the way things could be." When Jesus healed the blind man, he was showing his original audience, and us as well, that there could be a time when no one is blind. When he fed the five thousand, he was showing them there could be a time when no one was hungry.

We are to go and do likewise as Christ's disciples in the present age. We are to imitate him by working to bring about flourishing. We do this to show those within our spheres of influence the way things could be and point to the way things *will* be when Jesus returns to consummate his kingdom.

The work we do in the here and now is important to God. It serves as a signpost to point others to the new heaven and new earth, where all of God's children will one day live in perfect *shalom*. Until then, our calling is to work for the *shalom* of this present world to the glory of God, by the grace of God reweaving the unraveled fabric of our broken world.

The purpose of all our work as followers of Christ is to serve God's greater purpose for his creation. We have been called in our work to begin to repair, renew, and restore the "very good" of God's created world. T.M. Moore sums up this idea when he says:

> Our work only takes on full significance when we see it in this light, as part of
> God's ongoing work to bring everything to a higher state of goodness (Romans

8:28). So no matter what your job, or whatever your work might be, God intends that you should devote your labors to something greater than personal interest, economic prosperity, social good, or future beneficence alone. God intends your work to contribute to the restoration of the creation, and the people in it, to raising life on this blue planet to higher states of beauty, goodness, and truth, reflecting the glory of God in our midst. We will only fully appreciate the value and potential of our work when we see it in that light.[vi] ■

REFERENCES

i Gen. 1:10,1:12,1:18,1:25 (NIV).

ii Gen. 1:31 (NIV).

iii John R. Schneider, *The Good of Affluence: Seeking God in a Culture of Wealth* (Grand Rapids: Eerdmans, 2007).

iv Rev. 4:11 (KJV).

v Cornelius Plantinga, Jr., *Not the Way It's Supposed to Be: A Breviary of Sin* (Grand Rapids: Eerdman's, 1995) 10.

vi T.M Moore, "Work, Beauty, and Meaning: A Biblical Perspective on the Daily Grind" Breakpoint, https://www.breakpoint.org/features-columns/archive/1571-work-beauty-and-meaning

Reflection Questions:

1. What is shalom?

_____

_____

_____

_____

_____

_____

_____

_____

Reflection Questions continued:

2. How can you reweave shalom in your work?

_____

_____

_____

_____

_____

Discussion Questions:

1. God's response to his work on the sixth day was different from his responses to his work on the previous days. Why is this significant?

_____

_____

_____

_____

2. How is Jesus a model for reweaving shalom?

_____

_____

_____

_____

_____

3. How are the gospel and the cultural mandate connected?

_____

_____

_____

_____

_____

NOTES:

_____

_____

_____

_____

_____

_____

_____

_____

_____

_____

_____

_____

_____

NOTES:

The Sabbath Rest
Genesis 2:2-3, Exodus 20:8-11

We have seen in the opening chapters of Genesis that man was created by God for work.[i] For the Christian, life without work is meaningless, but work must never become the meaning of one's life. Work is one of the primary means by which we fulfill our true purpose: to glorify God, serve the common good, and further God's kingdom. God reminds us of this on the seventh day of creation.

At the end of the creation story we read:

> So on the seventh day he rested from all his work. Then God blessed the seventh day and made it holy, because on it he rested from all the work of creating that he had done.[ii]

God rested not because he was tired, but because he had completed his work.[iii] God wanted to teach us that work is not an end in itself, which is why he instituted the Sabbath. He reiterates this idea again in the Ten Commandments.[iv]

Today culture teaches that work is an end in itself. It is what supplies identity and meaning to our lives by maximizing success and money through our labor. Therefore, our work is never done, and the constant drive to prove ourselves destroys our ability to find rest.

This distortion of the purpose of work cripples our chances of finding true joy and fulfillment in our work. All work degenerates into pure, self-centered ambition when divorced from God.

How then does the Sabbath deliver us from always feeling stressed, exhausted, and running on empty?

One of the best explanations of the importance of the Sabbath to Christians today is found in an article written by Tim Keller a number of years ago.[v] Keller suggests it is not the physical work that exhausts us, but "the work under the work" that creates our unshakable weariness.

The only thing that will silence the condemning voices driving so many of us to the brink of exhaustion is the biblical discipline of what Keller calls "Sabbath rest."

Correctly practicing the Sabbath brings about a new spiritual understanding of both work and the whole of our lives. The purpose of Sabbath is not simply to rejuvenate yourself in order to do more. Nor is it only the pursuit of pleasure.

Instead, the purpose of Sabbath is to set aside time to enjoy:

- God.
- Joyful worship with God's people.
- God's glorious creation.
- Time with family.
- Life in general.
- Your accomplishments, achieved through God's help.
- The freedom found in the gospel, freedom from slavery to any material object or human expectation.

It is a time to unplug from our vocational work. The author of the book of Hebrews writes that we have to labor diligently to enter God's rest.[vi] We have to work hard at disconnecting from what we do the other six days and really enjoy the peace and release God has designed for us on this holy day. Sabbath keeping has to be intentional.

Setting aside one day in seven to observe the Sabbath will begin to change the way we see our work and what it can and cannot accomplish. This is why Jesus can tell his disciples,

Come to me, all you who are weary and burdened, and I will give you rest. Take my yoke upon you and learn from me, for I am gentle and humble in heart, and you will find rest for your souls. For my yoke is easy and my burden is light.[vii]

Thirteenth century poet Dante Alighieri wrote,

All our troubles, if we carefully see out their source, derive in some way from not knowing how to make a proper use of time.[viii]

We should love the vocational work that God has given us so much that he makes us take a day off every week. Let Sabbath rest rejuvenate you and your work. ■

REFERENCES

i   Gen. 2:15 (NIV).

ii Gen. 2:2-3 (NIV).

iii Gen. 2:2 (NIV).

iv Ex. 20:8-11 (NIV).

v   Timothy Keller, "Wisdom and Sabbath Rest" Q Ideas, http://qideas.org/articles/wisdom-and-sabbath-rest/

vi Heb. 4:11 (NIV).

vii Mt. 28:11-30 (NIV).

viii Rod Dreher, *How Dante Can Save Your Life: The Life-Changing Wisdom of History's Greatest Poem* (New York: Regan Arts, 2015).

Reflection Question:

1. What is the importance of Sabbath rest?

_____

_____

_____

_____

_____

_____

_____

Discussion Questions:

1. How does our culture distort our view of work?

_____

_____

_____

_____

_____

_____

Discussion Questions continued:

2. How does the concept of Sabbath rest inform our understanding of the mission of God's people?

_____

_____

_____

_____

_____

_____

_____

NOTES:

_____

_____

_____

_____

_____

_____

_____

_____

_____

_____

_____

NOTES:

NOTES:

Made in the USA
Middletown, DE
24 September 2015